"Carter's poems are about a sharply observed and often very passionately felt human present that is never seen or experienced apart from the past that preceded it, that haunts it, that gives it its resonance and life. Sometimes this is a personal past—a lost love, an unfulfilled possibility—but more often it is the longer historical and mythological human past, or an even longer past, 'a forgotten ontogeny, / like the memory of gills.'"

—R. H. W. DILLARD

"[These] poems are dense and smart. And they're odd, in a very pleasurable way. Each poem reiterates a particular kind of struggle with the dank, smelly, and entangled earth toward a transcendence that leaves us curiously uncertain whether the struggle has been into, or out of, form. Either the exquisitely careful crafting and the tendency toward meter and/or rhyme stand for the given mortal body we long to transcend, or else her craft itself *is* the transcendence, won from the swamp. She tells us, 'To bear divine love, we need / a certain passion for feathers and hair.' A fine and accomplished first book."

—FLEDA BROWN

The Memory *of* Gills

poems

the
memory
of gills

CATHERINE CARTER

C.C. Carter 9-28-07

To Michael,
whose service to
poetry has been
very great.
Thank you!
Catherine

LOUISIANA STATE UNIVERSITY PRESS
BATON ROUGE

Published by Louisiana State University Press
Copyright © 2006 by Catherine Carter
All rights reserved
Manufactured in the United States of America

An LSU Press Paperback Original
First printing

DESIGNER: Michelle A. Garrod
TYPEFACE: Tribute
TYPESETTER: The Composing Room of Michigan, Inc.
PRINTER AND BINDER: Data Reproductions, Inc.

LIBRARY OF CONGRESS CATALOGING-IN-PUBLICATION DATA

Carter, Catherine, 1967–
    The memory of gills : poems / Catherine Carter.
        p. cm.
    ISBN-13: 978-0-8071-3176-3 (pbk.: alk. paper)
    ISBN-10: 0-8071-3176-8 (pbk.: alk. paper)
    I. Title.
PS3603.A7769M46 2006
811'.6—dc22

                        2005031009

NATIONAL
ENDOWMENT
FOR THE ARTS

This project is supported in part by an award from the National Endowment for the Arts.

for

Margaret Anne Westbrook Carter
Worrall Reed Carter III

Contents

I

Sunken Tanks, Bloodsworth Island   3
The Last Good Water   4
A Long Way Inland   5
Evidence of Angels   6
The Stingrays   7
Letter Appealing a Citation   8
The Room Where Words Are   9
With the Net Down   10
Rapid Eye Movement   12
Witching Hour   13
The Ants and the Double Helix   14

II

Bury   17
Where the Dogs Lie   18
Early Elegy   19
Nine Lines for Some People I've Lost   20
The Telephone in My Dream   22
Narcissus Poeticus at the City Building   23
The Handsome Dentist Files Your Teeth   24
In the Mountains: An Occasional   25
Power Failure   26
Cthulhu in Atlantis   27
Hearing Things   28
Years Away: Paradelle for Diminishment   29
A History of the Lost Colony   30
Auspicious Days   31
For Malefactors Everywhere   32

III

Play Anything   35
On Having Once Been Hopelessly in Love on the
   Pennsylvania Turnpike   36
Nimuë, in the Magic Seminar   37

Leaving Love   38

The Semen Trees   39

The Day of the Summer Solstice   40

Two Years Married   41

Song for the Absent, with Hatchets   42

Semele's Story   43

Raised by Wolves   44

IV

Heart, Liver, Cormorant   47

Persephone Underground   49

Wingate, Maryland, Early Evening   50

Cullowhee Creek, After Thunder   51

This Brassiere   52

Meditation on Lettuce   53

The Other Story   54

The Fall   55

Galas Again   56

Because Forgetting Runs in the Family   57

Acknowledgments   59

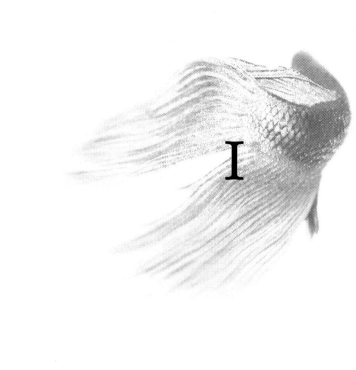

I

Sunken Tanks, Bloodsworth Island

The sand is gone, but the tanks are there
yet. Eight feet under, a hundred
yards out, a turret and a hatch
emerge, peer out, draw down
again. Edged iron gashes
the weight of murky water where it flushes
the crevices of the heavy treads,
the open lid, the view ports; rushes
through frothing; slaps
the rusted bolts. Mussels and the spat
of oysters set there, where the wash
of tide runs fast and high;
incurious eels scroll
past numb controls, a water-shattered gauge.
The bombers have gone home, and no one runs
strafing practice on the dead tanks now,
although—corroded lace—the three-inch gun
points south, across our bow.

The Last Good Water

By this spring you cannot stand
to drink like a man. If you would drink,
crouch on your muddy knees,
four-legged, or lie
flat to the ground, braced on wet hands
in the swale. Set your lips to clear
water, but shallow, not even
an inch. Move your dry
tongue to swallow, and taste oak leaves
and darkness. The spring
is a puddle that seeps
from the ground; dip it up
and you get mud. You must
be an animal here,
prostrate yourself. This spring will bear
no hand, no cup.

A Long Way Inland

At home now, up in small freshwaters
the strong skunk cabbages have been
the first swamp flowers. Where it's flatter,
downstream (miles) the salt soaks in
from open bay. *Spartina* grass,
I tell myself, might soon come on,
light as drift-fire, as chlorine gas,
that brilliant green—though it's too soon
by months yet for such vivid green
where salt is. So I'll have to hold
out for skunk cabbage, also green
as salt flame, sharp and brash and bold
enough to set the eye to thinking
the wetlands, without warning, burning.

But there's no such green here, no brink
of water quivering at the churn
of hip-boots—just the silver-vert
of white pines, yellow now as gilt
with cold and drought. There are dull skirts
of evergreens, the heavy belts
of fir. At home, where the flat lands
hide early growth in their low placid
folds, wild color marks the strands
of water: green like fire, like acid.

Evidence of Angels

Today I saw proof of souls.
I have evidence. I was out
teasing the buzzards—lying very still
to make them circle and look;
but they didn't land, though I lay for hours,
though they took the dog's mangled squirrel.
Scent, I thought; but I've seen them
stand waiting for quiet deaths;
or sight, but they find even the concealed.
So they must see souls, going out on the wind—
squirrel-souls jerking their ethereal tails,
deer-souls bounding the fields of air.
They saw mine, still stuck
at the edge of the skin, bound
like a book. I'm sending word
to Rome, that I've seen
the wings their dark robes mimic—
the resurrectors of the body,
real messengers of heaven,
swinging black and reeking from the sky,
watching the oily, hairy souls pull free.

The Stingrays

The love of God is a tricky business
if you don't like animals:
swans and snakes, bulls
and doves.
To bear divine love, we need
a certain passion for feathers and hair.
But God, it appears, hasn't yet plundered
his brother's demesne for an image,
nor come striding over the sea
to see the rays feed.

No one says she was stung
in the heart by that delicate barb;
no one was wrapped
in those brown silk wings,
or felt the diaphanous mouth
float down on her throat;
no one yet.

But sooner or later God assumes most forms,
in his rapist's passion for the world;
sooner or later, some ignorant woman,
happy in the bright sea,
will no doubt be struck
still by those great eyes,
will see the monstrous gill slits
shuttering open and closed
with the speed of divine pulse.

Sooner or later Zeus
and his blue-maned brother converge,
and the dark waves surround us,
and the slime-soft wings of rays
enfold us, and we fly swifter
than swans, softer
than doves.

Letter Appealing a Citation

It wasn't really reckless, unless
second gear on U.S. 301 (the backwoods stretch)
is reckless. I tried to tell him:
it was damp and slick
and the headlights fuzzed in the fog
and there were toads, hundreds
or thousands of toads,
all springing west. Their white throats flashed
like chips of quartz:
as if the headlights caught the song
inside, under the fretted, spotted,
invisible backs. I told him
I was swerving to miss them.
He said, *Ma'am, I'd like you*
to blow up this balloon. I told him
toads are an indicator species
for the resilience of the world—
canaries in the black mines—
every year declining.
He asked me how to spell my name,
told me I could appeal in writing,
which I am. If you see fit to rescind
my citation, you speak in favor
of mottled skins too bitter to eat,
splayed fingers fine as ferns
opening, those unlikely
trills, moving west
on the gleaming black road
in the rain—of that white flash
of song in the dark.

The Room Where Words Are

There aren't any walls.
The floor is pebble and sand,
the ceiling mercury—
heavy, hurrying, boiling silver.
Here inside, the lungs' snorkel
angles up to suck air,
while the original element
pours past, and the words—
like minnows, like tiny siblings
from a forgotten ontogeny,
like the memory of gills—
stare and start away.
They won't touch now;
this return becomes pursuit,
they are bait for my hooks,
snagged on my lines.

But it's so quick and quiet here,
so clean and sad. Once we were
the same, but now, too big, I strand
in the shallows, they flick
away: flame-bellied chub,
tessellated darter, vanishing
perfect word. I can't breathe
the original water. The room fills
with failure, I get thwarted and cold,
I wish I thought the finned words
understood, that I have to do
what I am doing. I rise
to my lungs and stand, hands sticky
with dead fish which can be cooked
to taste fresh, mounted
to look alive.

With the Net Down

For my part I should be as satisfied to play tennis with the net
down as to write verse with no verse form set to stay me.
—ROBERT FROST

To that I would have to reply that poetry is not a game.
—GALWAY KINNELL (PUBLIC LECTURE, 1989)

Both were right, both
wrong: we do love
our rules, and love
to break them, and Frost
did say
the work was play
for mortal stakes.
And the words are hard
as tennis balls, though lighter.
But love both the right
and the wrong as I will,
I remember other games: badminton
with my brother, summer
twilight, grass pale as straw,
leaves flickering.
Eleven and twelve, we batted
the white bird over and back,
dim and quick; even
while the rackets sprang holes
and the net fell down,
we kept on.
We'll say the net's here.
We'll call this the line.
A long way from town's asphalt courts
shaking with heat, the red-faced players
pounding and sweating,
the shredded bird flew
racket to racket, quiet and light
as a moth on the fading sky.

The bats of the summer evening
must have seen moths too:
they dipped and flittered over the net
of imagination and agreement,
stooped to the rise and drop
of the shuttlecock's pale wings,
and veered away, playing with us
the game of moths
and birds, where the rules
change, and go on changing.

Rapid Eye Movement

Navigation they say is science,
but on the bay it is dream:
the eyes' fast flutter
between chart pinned flat on the board,
compass flat in the hand,
and the round world rocking the hull and looking
like no chart ever drawn.
Says the chart, Gratitude Harbor;
the world is a hunched blue shoulder,
a bright bay saying
very little you understand.
Says the chart, Swan Creek,
where you see only a shadow
and no swans, not one,
where the chart's six safe sweet feet
are now the ominous scrape
of the world's harsh sand at your keel.

To make them merge you must enter the dream,
let the eyes start the stutter
from chart to world
while the scarlet needle swings between.
On a good trip, suddenly guess becomes knowledge,
blurred shoulder becomes harbor;
the nameless borrow names
from the word of the alien chart,

which, when it works, works.
The eyes flutter, the needle plunges
right round, the wind roars,
clocks and compass fall still, while you fly
back to the ramp, all the long way home,

where at last the eye stills. There
the mind shivers and wakens, there—
one foot poised on the gunwale, one
resuming the slope from water to earth—
the best dream ends, where the newly quiet
eye looks round at Gratitude.

Witching Hour

Not midnight, but twilight.
There's a black dog in the windy woods,
and other things: a clamor
of dogs across the river,
a barred owl calling hunger
and question from the swamp.
A whickering of sparrows settling
to quiet, and me, and a new
quarter moon in a spill of cloud.

Power is on the wind, and faith:
the owls are huddling chicks
through the darkness and ice
by the grace of blood.
Skunk cabbages shoulder up
through the trickling spring:
their striped frog-heads crack
through snow, waiting for the hatch
of the one fly that pollinates them.
They are sure it will come, sure
enough to trust everything
to the cold still coming.

Magic. More power than any witch
in Hawthorne could muster.
Round-based as a wine bowl, the quarter
moon tips light into the glowing cloud.
Springwater begins to gleam.
I kneel and swallow, and swallow
again; for now, there is still
more power, more water, and more.

The Ants and the Double Helix

With the cuttings of my nails
you can curse me, or by the ground
where my shadow lies. *Snick,*
a nail falls away, but witchery once
is science now: chains
of nucleotides bind the signature
of the self, and there they are
locked in horn, a thumb
print in every cell, all me.
Careful as we are
to keep ourselves intact
and singular, skin washed clean,
waste flushed away, nothing's
enough, no one is safe.
Where I pick at a scab, and a flake
of dry skin flicks to the grass, look—
the ants have gathered, it rocks
like a live thing, shimmers
with movement, one moment
of thousands where I scatter myself out,
becoming permeable to the world
that has a use for everything.
Ants nibble me cell by cell,
hoist me over antennae,
hurry me away underground.
They have me.
In synecdoche I am theirs
to feed upon, to curse, to bless.

II

Bury

A strange word. You can bury bulbs,
treasure, feelings, things in boxes. You cover
them under, and the dirt does its work,
which is of many kinds.
A strange word. It can rhyme
with *very,* and become succulent, thick
with black juice; seeds snap against your teeth.
And some places, south or west,
it doesn't do that in your mouth,
but sounds different; more like *hurry.*

Where the Dogs Lie

The real is what you can stand: the rocks
from the fallen fence hauled back
to the old plum orchard, to show
where the dead dogs lie; the way
the weeds grow over the rocks, and new
dogs come, and eventually lie there too.
That story's all right. It's the other
you can't take—the one
where the dogs are glossy again
and young, and running through fields
of camphor and horsemint where the rabbits
are finally slow enough, and no ticks
suck. That story makes you flinch
as no grave can. That story lies
hidden in the sorry heart,
buried like a dog itself, or waiting
like the baited carcass put out
by neighbors who hate dogs.
Sometimes, like a brown dog digging,
you paw those words, and taste. Hungry,
as dogs often are, you're tempted;
sometimes you eat. It's fine,
dead-sweet, for a while.
But by and by you're sorry, know
you should've let that story lie, when the sickness
of hope begins to move in the veins
and shiver under the skin: the unlikely
story, the poison
you ate in greed when it would
have been better to starve
and die, as the good dogs do.

Early Elegy

You're working up to dying. It is spring.
I don't mean to evoke that host of old
ironies and clichés (new life, your death,
juxtaposed by God's saturnine eye)
or comment on whatever this might say
about renewal. I just wonder how
you can unhand the world now, while it's March—
the light expanding, the rain on the glass,
the water-beaded weight of daffodils.
I don't know how you can, except you must,
apparently. If there's a lesson here
I hate it. Maybe if you hurt enough
you can let go of anything, stay in
the close room, let the daffodils go their
green way while you go yours.
Most likely, though, there is no lesson here
but strangeness. You are dying. It is spring.

Nine Lines for Some People I've Lost

THE LOST

There are more of you than there ought to be
by this time, like the white wound of a wake
behind me in the black impassive sea.
You pester me at night; you stand and rake
your fingers through my life, till I could cry.
So this is for you: something to break
open these griefs, which silence has let lie
and fester long enough. Come on. You make
me turn back now into the dark, and speak.

IN A YEARLY CARD

(to an almost-friend)

Did you ever forgive my losing you?
I loosed your hands from mine—perhaps I ought
not to have—when the hands I'd touched went through
my soft flesh, and left bruises. Maybe you knew
what you did (you can't say so); maybe not.
It doesn't make much difference, and you
are closed up now, a tough and tangled knot
for picking at. Try to forgive me, who
would like so much to love you, and cannot.

HOW ENDINGS HAPPEN

(for someone who cut her wrists)

I imagine that the bathroom light went out
while you sought something else. (You never said,
of course.) I think your fingers groped about,
as if they thought they might grow eyes, instead
of pulling back from the dark, where they fed
themselves on shapes. Your careful fingers thought:
I know it now. Here are the small Band-Aids
that never seem to cover up the cut,
and here the aspirin, here the razor blades.

IN NO LETTER

(for a friend I treated badly)

I know I never heard your middle name
or favorite color. All I really knew
was what you gave me: everything that came
while we were friends. Herb tea and *Dr. Who,*
and e. e. cummings, and the metro through
the underground. I don't know what to do
with them now, or with anger, or the shame
of loss. I can give nothing back to you,
whom I lost, due to all I never knew.

The Telephone in My Dream

Last night or rather this morning she called
on the telephone in my dream. She thought it was
Thanksgiving, and she didn't know she was dead.
I didn't want to tell her she was dead, or going to die
this May, which in the dream was still next May. I told her
about the job I still had last Thanksgiving,
tried to remember. My mother was there and spoke
to her; no one knew quite what to say
except *love*—and before that I woke up.
She called, across six months, six feet;
she called us, and we didn't know how to go
or what to say. *Dead* was too heavy, we couldn't
say that; we couldn't say anything really. Except *love,*
which this one time ought to have been enough,
but, as it always is, was nothing like enough.

Narcissus Poeticus at the City Building

They're still there,
though the sleeping garden was dozed under,
though the new wing had to be built.
They were planted and they naturalized,
year after year, hundreds of *Narcissus poeticus,*
white with the yellow eye and the heavy sweetness.
They are there now, underneath:
it takes them a year and more to die.
I know it's spring now,
when I begin to remember
how at first they are thirsty for light,
and then desperate; how they can't understand
what happened to the sun
that seemed like forever. How they push
and push against that ceiling of black stone.

The Handsome Dentist Files Your Teeth

with a tender-brutal hand
probes your slippery orifice,
sees the tongue, the spurting glands
that lubricate your words, your kiss,

the teeth where your skull's showing through,
the only part to be the same
when you're clean bone. This real you
is just his job. He'll lose your name

when you walk out. And while he's grinding
your teeth like a balky mule's
(his shy smile, like his spotlight, blinding,
blinding, too, his silver tools)

perhaps he's thinking of his wife
or mistress, or of wet bright moss
along a stream, where all the teeth
belong to trout, and need no floss.

Perhaps, while probes clink in his dish,
his cheek is pricked by misty rain;
he's reeling up a thrashing fish.

You look away. Spit down the drain.

In the Mountains: An Occasional

In the mountains an occasional
osprey loses his way
to the branch over this
branch, this shallow
hard-floored river. Sometimes
I see one there, far-flung
from the brown estuaries,
the pearl-shine of salt
and fluster of foam. Sometimes
the bird seems charged by that place
with a message, some word
from home—a foreign word
now, scrawled in froth
and feather, the hieroglyphs
of scale and scute. *Remember,*
it may say, *though you stab*
down roots like claws
into these long levels
and planes of granite, remember
the cormorants fishing, the realm
of water. Or maybe
(in translation emphasis
is everything)
it's the other way: *Though*
you remember skates'
wings and three-square
sedge and black
needle rush, you need fish,
and you can fish;
there are fish here.
I don't know which
it is, only that it is:
the hawk-cry of hunger,
word of home.

Power Failure

November 3, 2004

My office, at the end of the hall, has a window,
a west window, open to rain.
That silver light pours down the hall:
past my corridor-mate reading on the floor
in the dim gleam from this window,
to the cross-corridor lying in pale shadow,
to the bathroom across the way, all but black.
In the bathroom I can just see the taps,
thin as the ghosts of hopes that died hard.
In the near-black I draw water.
The light I use comes from the window:
not sunlight, not incandescence, not
really enough, though it runs a long way—
not much, but without it
this long hall would be blind;
having light means letting light go
as far as it will, it means opening the door.

Cthulhu in Atlantis

My mind lies like Cthulhu in Atlantis;
a foam-washed minaret, a weedy dome
of consciousness or reason peering out
are iceberg points above a waste of trough
and crest and trough. Far underneath, the rest:
the hills and valleys of the sunken city—
desire, hunger, attics, roofs, who knows
what's down there, what the dead ones built and shaped
from hardware, software, nightmare, voices, books,
more books? White on the maps, with dragons' heads:
that's right too, for there are monsters here,
at least one monster, sleeping in the cellar
a slimy sleep, as it dreams of the night
the mystery rises through the waters, streaming
salt and venom. (*Finding Lost Atlantis*!
proclaims Discovery Channel, as if this
were such a good idea.)

When I awake
to rainlight in the morning, coffee, cream,
conundrums of the office, furnace warmth,
sometimes I think the turrets sank too far
in sleep and I returned to that deep place,
and I remember. Just a little, but enough:
remember wandering in flooded rooms,
obsidian water flushing through the gills
this place requires, or remember weed
like rotted hair. And somewhere in the lost
place lie the dead things that are never dead:
gelatinous Cthulhu, and its power
to poison, or to swamp, those slender spires
that rise above the ceiling into day
with everything that's otherwise obscure:
with stone-locked water and the liquid silt
of centuries, with kelp and octopi,
and jellyfish and urchins and the shoals
of silver reef-fish, and the wicked mouths
of moray eels thrashing in the light.

Hearing Things

I have begun to hear things. The lettuce
stem, the potato peel, the rind of lemon—
Don't throw us away, they beg.
Don't embalm us in the landfill
where everything stinks and seeps
together; we want
to be leaves again, and breathing
threads of roots. We want it all,
everything. Thinking of the hole
in the hill lidded and simmering, taut
as an angry boil, I quail. I obey
the word of apple cores; I carry
the scraps to the field, I do
what is asked. But the voices
do not stop. The rattlesnake
plantain on my parents' farm lifts its flat
white-veined dark leaves: *Keep*
the backhoes from this land. You can
protect me. The dog at the shelter:
Unlatch the gate: I will be good!—And I don't
know how to answer, what
to say. There are these voices. I am
hearing things.

Years Away: Paradelle for Diminishment

Years away, for nights at a time, invisible birds wept *whippoorwill.*
Years away, for nights at a time, invisible birds wept *whippoorwill.*
Whippoorwill, we all whistled back the lost and tenor dark.
Whippoorwill, we all whistled back the lost and tenor dark.
All away back to the dark invisible year, we wept
for time and tenor lost, nights of whistling birds: *whippoorwill, whippoorwill.*

Years away, shoals of mussels plowed the pebbles of the river bed.
Years away, shoals of mussels plowed the pebbles of the river bed.
Bluegills, glinting-scaled, nipped them broken-shelled from our hands.
Bluegills, glinting-scaled, nipped them broken-shelled from our hands.
The broken mussel shells glinting, bluegills nip the scaled pebbles
for beds from the plowed shoals, our hands years away from them.

Almost no one alive now remembers the years of shad runs, that, how
    many? came.
Almost no one alive now remembers the years of shad runs, that, how
    many? came.
Years since they surged up the river, when the shallows seethed away at
    their splash.
Years since they surged up the river, when the shallows seethed away at
    their splash.
How many alive remember the shad coming up? seethe and surge at these
    shallow
years when almost no one runs to their rivers? Years away, now, that splash.

Almost no one seethes and weeps for nights, years of birds,
rivers' surge, the shad runs coming from shoals of pebbles, whippoorwills
(that whistling's scaled tenor! *whippoorwill*) mussels' shells, the bluegills' nip
and splash away in glinting riverbeds—for the almost-lost to our hands,
all alive then. And how many years back-broken now, invisible in time
ploughed up from them? We remember, years away.

Billy Collins invented the "paradelle" (although for some time he called it an old French form).
Each of the first three stanzas requires a line that immediately repeats itself, another that does the
same, and then two more lines that use all of the words of the first and third lines, and no others.
The final stanza uses all of the words from the first and third (or, if you like, the final two) lines
of each stanza and no words that those stanzas do not use.

A History of the Lost Colony

In the alluvial plain beneath the refrigerator
we did well; food was abundant, the soft
rains dripped. But we needed *Lebensraum:*
our cup ran over, our downy children
crowded together. So we sent
the colony: filamentous explorers, our dearest
spores, a sister city under the cliff
of the outer grille. The light there
was muted; the ooze was regular,
nourishing, fragrant with decay.
At first, good reports: hyphae
expanded the borders of a town round
as a drop of rain, mycotoxins ready
to repel invaders. The seers saw
only prosperity; the auspices taken
from the shaking of the earth were good.
How could we know?
Who could foresee the blasting of those soft
heads, those feathery arms?
who could imagine that ocean
falling, that splash
of acid from the sky? A yard away
we heard the screaming.
The world stank of bleach, reeked
of chemical burns. Our brethren writhed
inside out, shriveled in agony. *Colony,*
colony! We clutched each other
in dactylic grief, our poisoned children
gone in a swipe of cloth.
We do not know
why it happened. What thread of God
we angered, why the signs lied, what
wrong we did. Now when we think
of our new colony, on a tender island of potato
fallen between the wall and the toaster,
we are afraid. No one
is safe. The world is a desperate place.

Auspicious Days

What is it about blood? You never
saw a day like this—the clarity
that makes you laugh with pleasure:
the sky stranded between blowing leaves,
the champagne light
that makes the college girls
look perfect, joyous, sane.
This morning the cat caught
a yelping rabbit, whose skin
shucked off like a glove when I tried
to break its neck, whose blood
rushed hot and fetid over my hands.
And this day!
For centuries we poured blood over stones
for days like this,
pleasing to gods and men.

For Malefactors Everywhere

Some people take to crime, but didn't mean
it to work out that way. It started small:
that leaf-blade knife from Kenya you weren't sure
you ought to have, the foreign currency,
the alien seed, the fruit fly on the fur
of an illicit peach that got through free.
But it went on, to more ambitious hauls:
the contraceptive drugs, the worn blue jeans.
You live like that: you like the shady side.

You falsify your passport, not to show
the places where you've stashed your smuggler's heart.
There are some things you never will declare:
bigger than ice-packed kidneys, or the parts
for foreign motorcycles. You've been scared
forever, always worried what to hide,
what's safe to show. And some things never are.

III

Play Anything

Like almost everyone, I find it hard
to resist a musician, or actually anyone
smooth enough to make something look easy,
as this one guy could; this one sweet-
tempered light-eyed keyboard player,
bass player, pretty much everything player,
the one to whom three of us sent anonymous love
letters for a couple of months, mostly
to make him happy since he made us
so happy, though also for the chance to write
things like *Your eyes are blue tide pools*
in which barracuda swim to snap at my heart
(which is not something you get to write just
every day); the guy I really fell for, though, only
when he fingered the keys on a squally old
flea-market accordion, and I said, *You can play that?*
and he said, truly, *I can play anything.*

On Having Once Been Hopelessly in Love
on the Pennsylvania Turnpike

Billows of anise, brilliant chartreuse, blew in the breeze of the last
morning in June, after I saw him the last
time. That morning! By ten I had come down the long slopes
again into the mid-Atlantic meadowlands,
the light clear and the wind flowing easy,
and there in the grassy hills the roads were fringed
with wild anise, tossing its umbels,
shaping the air with licorice. It was
some kind of miracle, a new morning in the world,
since I was a little in love, and with no hope
to taint delight with plans or longings. Love
without hope—a wonderful thing,
a gift from an oblivious beloved. It is a theft
never reported, like light stolen
from the sun: and the sun doesn't miss it, light
being what the sun does, and what it is, and if—
like the anise, like everything—your veins
run chlorophyll, you love the light, loving it
makes you glad. The world was sweeter
for the anise's joy, and mine, even when, today,
the office gardeners cut back the anise,
dried on its empty stalks, and gone to seed.

Nimuë, in the Magic Seminar

I watch you all the time. I want to tie
you down and suck you dry.—That sounds obscene.
It is, of course, though not the way you mean;
you're right to be offended, it's not love,
exactly. But be honest—you don't want
me either; with us it's all what you know,
and what I don't. It's all that you could say
if you would. It's the art you've used your life
to light, and I've used mine to want. You could
say everything: *See, this is my nonce form,*
this, amphibrachic blank tetrameter
with trochees alternating! You could say,
This was by ear or *I can show you how*
to shape a step that makes the slow foot light.

But will you? Can you really tell it all,
or understand how magic cries for spells?
If not—if there's no password—then look out.
You'll find me some late evening in your bed.
I'll touch you, if it seems I must, and lust
will be quite real. But I'll lie waking after;
I'll listen. I'll lean over you, I'll wait
to hear you mumble half a line, one magic
word. I'll take it all down—oh, you know
I will, and who knows better why I must?
Merlin, spare us what I'll do for greed—
the lies, the dreams of oakwood.

                              Tell me what I need.

Leaving Love

Maybe you cry a little, take a lot of last
looks, like at the beach when you were
small: throwing out jars still half full
of mustard or raspberry jam, taking the last
crusts of bread down the sand for the gulls,
saying, *No, this was beautiful, this was our*
dune, our sea oats, won't we see the dolphins
one more time, good-bye, good-bye!
And the drive away is long, hot, your house
when you finally get there in the late
afternoon fusty, full of thirsty fleas that have drunk
nothing for a week. You think of the wind
and sand, the sweets you never get
the rest of the year, and your heart shrinks.
Unpacking's worse than packing, somehow,
and everyone's tired and cross, no one says
how good you were to give it all up, come back.
But the next morning is a little better;
the windows are open again, you've lain
in your own bed, hugged the dogs who dumbly
mourned you for a week, and look,
it's August, here are your books, it's time
to wash clothes (though you keep one towel
out, to smell the salt), time to come home,
wake in the summer morning to mow
the lusty grass, weed the tomatoes and beans,
let go, take hold, bang open the rusty
screen door back into your own days.

The Semen Trees

Smells like—virgins. Lots and lots of virgins.
—DAN K., ON NOTICING THE POLLEN

In the northeast in June something blooms
whose pollen smells of semen.
Up it comes around you: air suffused
with warmth, salt, that
bland weight of scent, until you
stop, suspicious and alarmed,
refusing: it can't
be. Furtively you sniff
your fingers, check yourself
for stain, wonder if this morning
has made itself plain.
It hasn't. This is more.
This is the world
grown vascular and languid;
these lumens and pores of joy
are not yours
alone.—You may never discover
what wells into the air, changing breath
to breaches cells can swim.
It may be trees with heavy-hanging
bells, or weeds' granular stamens
that swell the day with semen,
but it is ambient: the alien
world of chlorophyll, those green
veins, gone suddenly human.

The Day of the Summer Solstice

The pond is duckweed green. Queen Anne's lace
froths in my hands, and the whippoorwill
today sang grace in the early light
for the year's full tide, the still
lull of the long day.
My glance touches yours,
in the day's damp heat under the tall willow,
and our voices, when we speak, are unsteady.
Two friends wait ready; edgy fingers hold gold.
In the quiet we hear bullfrogs break off
and begin again, the mutter of ducks,
the whisper of breath and cloth
where nearly everyone we love is listening.
The sun at the height of its haste is poised
for the turn toward cold, but not
yet. It is the longest day still—
the throb of frogs, the hour of the Queen
Anne's lace and the eye-blue cornflowers—the place
where everything has paused,
thrumming: flesh made word, high summer.

Two Years Married

The long grass is alive again. Woodchucks
rise out of it on their strong haunches,
palms folded as if they never
devoured a garden or honeycombed a field
into a livestock death trap, eyes alert
for something succulent, something
different. They are made to go
on four legs, to peer up from between
their brown shoulders close to the earth,
not to make the targets of themselves
they do make as they stand to look
out over the grasslands, perilous
to the tender world, imperiled in it.
The ground is enough, and more than enough;
it's where they live and eat and mate,
give birth to the young as charming
as they are destructive, all eyes and hands
and sleek faces you'd like to pet
if you didn't know how lithe and fierce
they have been before, and are now.
But still they rise out of it, earth
and young and all, and pause to look,
to look around: for something different,
dangerous, something to destroy, something
to destroy them, to eat them away from earth.
I stand looking back, tall on my legs.
I think of falling in love again —
for a moment or two, just one more time.

Song for the Absent, with Hatchets

When you're gone, one
hatchet murderer (hatchet included), one
syphilitic serial rapist slitting my screens, one
anti-environmental militiaman complete with M-16, one
madman who gnaws his victims' spleens
while defiling, with semen, their dead hair—one
is not enough. No, all of them,
all and then some, creep near
my lonely house together. Alive or not,
Manson is there; nor do Hannibal Lecter or Norman
Bates let their fictional nature keep them away.
—Now they are playing, drawing straws, having fun,
dividing with scrupulous justice
the minutia of torture (*fingernails for you,*
eyes for me), considering: *First, make her run. . . .*
Of course they evanesce
with the climb of the sun. But this is one
of the many things I hate about having you gone.
                              If you were here none
of it could happen. Your voice, your soft snore,
drive the killers in my mind away downhill, to
some other county where everyone lies alone.
Creatures of loneliness, they would shiver
in dread at the scent of your skin, never
dare brave the haze of warmth our two
bodies breathe together in the covers, afraid to
ever crawl out of my safe skull, draw near us two.

Semele's Story

. . . she asked Jove for a favor, and did not name it.

. . . .

And doomed to die on that account, she responded:
"Come to me as you come in love to Juno!"
—OVID, *Metamorphoses,* BOOK III, TRANS. ROLFE HUMPHRIES

She was flash-fried like a sweet
potato, she sparkled and spat
sparks, she was blinded in that blind
river of power pouring
down the sky; the blue-white
ozone arc welded
her flesh to the floor. *No
more,* she might have cried,
too late, as the electrical caul
illuminated her face—lashes
and teeth flickering, blazing—as fit
to split the sky he groaned as he came,
in grief, or pleasure; and she died.
Too late. She had said
what she said.

Come to me as the thunder.
Nudged by a jealous wife,
it is true; but she knew.
We say it too;
Batter my heart (or anyway some
part) said one whose name
meant *give.* And when the gift
batters us half dead—well, we said
what we said: what Semele said
to Zeus, and most of us
to the world, and I, sometimes, to you:
*I don't care, let me know, come
as the thunder.* Sometimes
the world does; and sometimes (you
see these burns) you do.

Raised by Wolves

Don't think the move to town didn't take:
like Mowgli, I married human.
Like the seal-girls, I was glad,
though they can't live too close to the dunes
and I prune the woods from my yard,
rake up the leaves that rustle and hiss
like paws under moon-gray trees.
I married human, and since I was
after all speciously human too,
they said it seemed like fate,
even the wolves. When I visit the den,
we nuzzle and scratch each other
(that opposable thumb, so handy),
ask why humans live in pieces,
why they use air machines
on such cool nights, if we're the last
wolves; since the new strip mall,
we've seen no more. Then
I lope for town, pause at a roadkill:
possum, sweet as persimmon but rank
with burst bowels and feces. In the suburbs
I catch a cab. In the house again, I circle
twice and snuggle against my spouse;
at this hour he's most like a wolf.
If I dream of veins, it's his neck
my blunt fangs catch, but I learned
in the woods how to mate for life,
though the mate is different. Don't think
I feel sorry for myself, or him: those years
in the leaves were the meat of my life,
and everyone marries into another species.

IV

Heart, Liver, Cormorant

Heart. I hate,
sometimes, that metaphor
so used no one knows it is:
that thick red thoughtless
muscle thudding its one
(*life*) word (*life, life*) again,
again, again, three or four
billion times per life,
that heart now the seat
of all Western affection, all grief.
In old China it was liver:
You are wedged in my liver,
or *You have broken*
my liver. But no, here
always the heart.
It is vital in its stubbornness
and stupidity, its one
desperate word, and while
it says *life* so often it has
no sense, it does not say
I love, I break, or *Look, that light*
at the river mouth! or anything
else except, perhaps, that
it hates arterial plaque.
Whatever clutches and bites
its lip at the early light
on flat water, the black cormorant
driving low and fast and steady
as a heart itself, it is not
the heart; I don't know
what it is. Perhaps
there is something in there
no one has seen, so that when
I see that spreading gleam again,
that drill-beat of wings,
I can resist the still-there

urge to murmur, *Oh,*
my heart, say instead,
My liver,
my cormorant,
you quick wings against my ribs, my skull.

Persephone Underground

Nobody says it isn't terrible, it is
terrible, splitting open and feeling darkness
pour into you, it is what you think it is,
violation, none worse. But don't you remember
who he is? You can't avoid him. You can't
stay indoors, or lock him up. I married
death, and after it was over and only
beginning, in the dark I started to see:
it's what he's like. And he loves me,
in his way: in the way
that he loves everyone, that he loves
you. Down here, you can see
yourself: part of a harem drawn together
from every living breath, every last
desire. Even as he clenches his fingers
in my hair he's beckoning other
lovers; his kiss touches everywhere
at once. You think that I picked some
shining fool's narcissus, from which you
can refrain. But he's a patient lover.
He'll prolong it, wait for you
a while; he'll court you, murmur
your name through the dark hedges
at night, give you time to feel
the shiver of his hand. I know
you won't believe, up there in the bright
hours, but you're dreaming of him
too; you're promised to him too,
and all at once, tonight's the wedding night.

Wingate, Maryland, Early Evening

It's not the end of the world,
but you can see it from here,
warns the sign on the one store.
You can see it.
Flat beneath the sand-
paper rub of the sun,
this end of everything lies
wearing away. In the slips hulls
go gray as salt; curls
of paint bend back, peel
into the silty sloughs. The wind
is sweet with decay
fathoms deep: grass stalk, snail shell,
narrow fecal trails, mud fertile
as milt. At the end of the world
and the day, the green-headed flies
hum thirstily after blood; like small men
with large shields, the fiddler crabs
tend their burrows, scramble the tidal mud.
The sun throbs down, the marsh
drinks heat, a few more inches
of the sun-scoured town
evaporate. As ends go
it isn't bad: the heat,
the endless light, the wear
into air and silt, the lively
small things never noticing
the end always
going on,
still
going on.

Cullowhee Creek, After Thunder

Force is measured in foot-pounds; force
jams the trout lily up
past gravel. It is force
against which the stride pulls
and fails, pulls
and fails, and the slow force
of burn which drives the stride
forward—the never-
resting never-ended work
of work. This flood:
the work of water over rock is met
by a white spate back, so strong
that the stream is hoarse with silt,
wicked with sticks, torn
earth, drowned worms. But it is not
wicked—the rough
caress which combs the long grass
like harsh hair—nor,
no matter what I call it, is it a touch,
though some touches are like it.
This flood is power,
the energy of the world
grinding away at the energy
of the world, the thing you feel
when what you want—
when all you want—
is work.

This Brassiere

has something—fastener, buckle,
gasket, block and tackle—which creaks: a dry
peaceful voice as I walk, the sound
of a windsock tugging its rope, a boat
at anchor, lifting and lilting to some soft swell,
to the admittedly pelagic sway of breasts
like the swell and swing of salt
water. Landlocked, lacking buoyancy and specific
gravity, they are heavy in their slow shift
and murmur of wire and line. But not forever:
when I am dead, spare them the chatoyance of fire
or depravity of casket. Instead find a ship
in need of a bowsprit, a figurehead,
a deep-breasted salt-streaked gull-spattered
girl up front, storm and calm, cleaving
horizon, leaving everything behind.
Wood is more usual, but with embalming,
what is impossible? So nail me up there,
shriveled, antique, but creaking
all the way home, find some last sailor
who can't afford a woman of teak, and let it go on
till I mummify and the beaks have pecked me
down to bone: *creak, creak, creak.*

Meditation on Lettuce

The lettuce does not want to be the lettuce
we know—succulent, riffle-edged,
green to the tongue, moist
and fresh as the cheek of a child.
The lettuce wants more; that stalk
cries out to stretch, to lengthen
into a tower, a scepter, a spurt
of flowers, a spatter of seeds,
its humid leaves yearn to turn
to thorny spears, jagged blades.
It thinks, if lettuce can think,
of the day it will have met
its purpose, and can stand emptied
out, withering, desiccated, fulfilled.
But I will not have it.
Brutal knife in hand I take
to the garden, I snick off the full
heavy stalk, I demand
a head. I thwart the lettuce
in its climb to power and peace,
I insist that it remain full, potential,
a Lolita of lettuces,
turgid, prepubescent, delicious.
Let us be forgiven our hunger, our lust,
out of which, lettuce, I have sinned against you.

The Other Story

The folding web below
my thumb is growing. Other
skin slackens and creases,
bristles spring from my chin,
fat grows harder
to combat. No doubt
you'll call this age,
or sloth, but I know
better. These are signs.
No one would say
where Grandma went, or Aunt
Cornele, but I can guess,
now that I am becoming a seal.

Yes. I forgo my thumbs,
I am standing in the surf,
now falling forward, now
flying. (Forty years
ago he gave me pearls,
a sign of water, not
wealth; certain tears
were only the pledge of salt.)
Alewives, leaping pale
in the phosphorescent sea,
moon on the climbing breakers,
wait for me—my spotted skin,
my fused fingers—any night
now I'll be there.

The Fall

One afternoon when he was seven, rocking
on the porch rail spelling out words about stars,
his hooked-in heel slipped, and he pitched back
into the grass. When he could look, the lawn's
low clover was like something in his book:
a vast reach thick with clusters, sweeps of stars,
he thought, and winged things tending stars,
carrying bright dust the short way between
the stars' white tremors. It was only
the usual thing, pain, which told him
he wasn't dead, that these were not
angels (which he knew about from Sundays)
touching stars into shine. Only hurt
whispered to him that this world
was his world, that these were bees
not angels, that the yards all white
with clover were not the fields of heaven.

Galas Again

In September apples that were
sweet like water turn tart
like wine; the slack
and mealy are reborn. They grow
hard as good muscle, as sharp
cider, as new lovers;
as your own lover suddenly
leaf-fire bright again. In their
crisp skin you taste saffron
leaves sailing the twilight
sky, smell yellow pencils
sharpened into new youth,
a shorter one this time.
This is the new year,
you think, as the air
begins to change, as death
just brushes the world, and what
wouldn't you give for one more
apple the equal of this?

Because Forgetting Runs in the Family

You know me now.
Someday, I know, you won't.
Someday I'll have to say, all over
again: *It's all right. Don't*
try too hard to know.
It's only family,
chromosome-kin
to your mind, your bones.
Sometimes I feel alone
now, but not
like I will then. Now
is now, and now
what I can't hold I have:
your voice sure on my name,
when I come to the jamb of home
in the whole certainty of being
recognized. Known.

Acknowledgments

The author gratefully acknowledges the editors of the following publications, in which some of the poems in this book first appeared, sometimes in slightly different form: *Chiron Review:* "The Stingrays"; *Cider Press Review:* "Cullowhee Creek, After Thunder," and "Meditation on Lettuce"; *Comstock Review:* "Where the Dogs Lie" (as "Where the Dogs Are Buried"); *Evansville Review:* "Play Anything"; *Faultline:* "The Last Good Water" and "In the Mountains: An Occasional"; *Georgia State Review:* "For Malefactors Everywhere"; *Graffiti Rag:* "Evidence of Angels"; *Louisville Review:* "Cthulhu in Atlantis" and "The Day of the Summer Solstice"; *Main Street Rag:* "Power Failure"; *Mudfish:* "Letter Appealing a Citation"; *North Carolina Literary Review,* "The Ants and the Double Helix"; *Phoebe: An Interdisciplinary Journal of Feminist Scholarship:* "Witching Hour"; *Poetry:* "The Fall"; *Potomac Review,* "Wingate, Maryland, Early Evening"; *The Southern Anthology: "Narcissus Poeticus* at the City Building" (as "Poeticus Narcissus at the City Hall"); *Tor House Foundation Newsletter:* "Persephone Underground."